W9-CWE-856

Youth Ministry:

Sunday, Monday, and Every Day

Youth Ministry: Sunday, Monday, and Every Day

John L. Carroll and
Keith L. Ignatius

Judson Press® · Valley Forge

YOUTH MINISTRY: SUNDAY, MONDAY, AND EVERY DAY

Copyright © 1972
Judson Press, Valley Forge, Pa. 19481
Seventh Printing, 1977

Library of Congress Cataloging in Publication Data

Carroll, John L.
    Youth ministry: Sunday, Monday, and every day.
    1. Church work with youth.   I. Ignatius, Keith L.,
joint author.   II. Title.
BV4447.C37   268'.4   72-3236
ISBN 0-8170-0577-3

Printed in the U.S.A. ⊕

The name JUDSON PRESS is registered as a trademark in the U.S.
Patent Office.

Contents

MARK ME UP!

Help me become your book. Read me with a pencil in hand. When you find something that gives you an idea, mark a big **!** , **★**, or **®**. When you see an idea that really turns you off, write **BLAH !**

When you come to a section that you want to return to, read again, and think about the ideas it contains, put a big circle around it like this.

Write notes in the margin like

These writers are really out of it !

or

This may even work in our group !

So tell the story of your reading with marks **★ ! ®** or make up some that make sense to you.

Introduction
What Is Youth Ministry?

Youth ministry is the "whole world"! The whole world of the youth and adults who are caught up in the give and take, ups and downs, excitement and depression that make up that which we call life.

Youth ministry takes place "Sunday, Monday, and every day." It has broken out of the church school classroom, out of the fellowship group, and into the world — the whole world.

This is not to say that youth ministry no longer takes place in the church school classroom or in the fellowship group. It simply is found in other places like the kitchen at home, the English class at school (and the hallways and free times in that school), the walks with a friend, or the job to earn money.

All these places and times become the scene for youth ministry.

Youth ministry means more than the age group characterized as "kids," "youth," "young people," "adolescents," "they," etc. It means younger brothers and sisters, parents, and other adults who care. They, too, are caught up in youth ministry when their lives intersect the lives of youth.

Youth ministry is carried on in and through the church. Everybody is involved. It's not limited to the kids and their sponsors. The decisions the deacons and all the other committees make about how your church will function will determine what happens in youth ministry.

This book is an attempt to think about what needs are a part of youth ministry today.

It talks about

- A philosophy of youth ministry rooted in the gospel, calling for congregational commitment, "shooting down" myths, and defining success.

- What we need to do and how we do it by looking at and discovering needs,

  resources, and

  responses.
- Leadership,

  asking that we take seriously the leadership needs (for quality of leadership determines whether we sink or swim).

  pointing out the kinds of adults that the church must put in contact with youth.

  describing ways of recruiting and readying adults for leadership roles.

  calling youth to give leadership to "their thing."
- Organization,

  the last topic to be considered because organization grows out of knowing what we want to do and what's available with which to do it.

That's what this book is all about.

Youth ministry: Sunday, Monday, and every day.

1
A Philosophy of Youth Ministry

This book is put together on the assumption that those who pick it up have a concern for youth ministry in their congregation. Some who read it will be planners, others implementers. In many churches the roles are merged — you plan it and you do it!

The book deals with administering youth ministry in and through the congregation. It's concerned with ORGANIZATION — how you can go about the job.

But to talk about organization without putting in a bit about PHILOSOPHY (concepts) could make talking a pretty meaningless effort. We would end up going around in circles in an organizational stew. We need to understand *why* we do *what* we do!

The theory and practical suggestions in these pages have been brought together so that youth ministry in your church will take on the meaning everybody hopes for it to have. Okay? Let's go!

Let's try a definition of this term "youth ministry." Youth ministry is all of that which takes place for and with youth in and through the local church.

All of these and more are part of youth ministry.
- church school class
- pastor counseling a senior high
- youth group meeting
- "help line" on youth problems
- public school teacher expressing commitment through teaching

Youth ministry is a comprehensive term, gathering in whatever efforts a church might make because of a concern for youth. There are many varieties of response or action in the youth ministry picture. The sections on organization and program will talk about varieties in more detail.

FOUNDATIONS: ROOT, TASK, AND FOCUS

THE ROOT OF YOUTH MINISTRY IS THE GOSPEL.

- We matter. As individuals and as the race of man, we are of incalculable worth to God.
- We are loved. The supreme example of this kind of love is found in the Christ event. We see what shape love takes in the life, death, resurrection, and ongoingness of Christ.
- We are to love each other " — as I have loved you" [John 15:12], reaching out across uncertainties into caring relationships.
- Because we matter, because we are loved by God, and because we are enabled to love each other, we give thanks to God for his gift of life.
- Gratitude for God's freely given gifts of love and life makes us want to live out our lives in faithful response, joyous obedience, and liberating trust. This commitment becomes the freely chosen basis for our particular life-styles as Christians.[1]

THE TASK OF YOUTH MINISTRY IS TO EQUIP YOUTH FOR MISSION IN THE WORLD — to bring the reality of the gospel into relevant encounter with youth in their life situations.

- How can the Christian faith help youth decide what they value and where they can find meaning in a confused world?
- In what ways can the Christian faith help youth overcome their anxieties and fears?
- What is there in the Christian faith that can help youth joyously affirm life and its challenges?
- How does a Christian young person decide what is an acceptable, wholesome sexual expression?
- What are Christian perspectives on pollution, the population explosion, responsible citizenship, and other enormous social problems?

[1] Sheila Campbell, *Your Ministries with Senior Highs* (Nashville: Board of Education of the United Methodist Church, 1971), pp. 14-15. Used by permission.

- How can the Christian faith help youth combat racism at school, class prejudice in a community, and other forms of crippling discrimination?[2]

THE FOCUS FOR YOUTH MINISTRY IS NOW! Once the task of youth "work" in the church emphasized the training of youth for *future* leadership roles. Today's youth generation is saying the future is *today*. We need to give leadership — now; respond to issues — now; influence those decisions that shape our lives — now. (You know this really isn't in conflict with future leadership roles. Youth will be better leaders tomorrow because they have been in leadership roles *now*.)

So the focus is now. We deal with personal and social life issues of youth, confronting these issues with the meanings of the gospel.

Now you've got some theory that you need to remember.

Youth ministry is *all* that the congregation does *for and with youth*.

Youth ministry is *rooted* in the *gospel*.

Youth ministry equips youth for *mission* in the *world*.

Youth ministry deals with *now*!

Don't forget these points. Those who do, organize in vain!

FACE REALITY

One of the most helpful steps you can take in planning is to de-mythologize youth ministry in your church.

A myth is a person or thing existing only in the imagination — whose actuality is not verifiable.

Youth ministry takes place in a real world – not in a wish world. Planners and implementers need to understand and consider that fact.

Some myths:

- Every church except yours is "successful" with youth.

[2] *Ibid.*, p. 15.

- Youth ministry is easy (and you can't understand why you can't make it go).
- All youth are the same, all churches the same, and hence the same thing should work everywhere.
- "Good" programs are the answers.
- Youth are eager to respond to your offerings.
- Some day, in some way, you and your church will be "successful" with kids.

Let's get youth ministry out of a dream world. Let's see it in reality — in practicality. The fact is you're not programming for a computer, arranging your groceries in a refrigerator, or training your dog. Youth ministry is not simply a program. It is a willingness to share in the life struggle of an adolescent. Remember your own struggle — the ups and downs, moods, excitements, and all the rest. How on earth do you program for that? To try to program for a collection of senior highs who are at various stages, affected by a mass of influences (school, parents, love, peers, pimples, and appearance), is a mild form of insanity. To assume that all will be moved on Sunday at 6:15 P.M., to become ecstatic over one subject is a bit presumptuous.

Quite the contrary. But if you learn to enter into the struggle, accept the changes, be human yourself, get angry when you need to, throw up your hands when it's in order, and smile when you feel like smiling, you'll have a great time.

So now that you have got some more theory, be realistic about what you face and what you can do in youth ministry.

WHERE IT HAPPENS

Youth ministry happens in the context of a local congregation. Administration of youth ministry in your congregation requires answers to the following questions:

1. What priority does youth ministry have in your church?
2. How well have you interpreted youth ministry to the congregation as a whole? Do *they* know what you're about?
3. What assistance and support do you expect from the congregation as a whole?

4. Have you a clear understanding of what the youth committee expects of adult workers with youth and what the adult workers expect of the committee?
5. What role do youth play in planning and directing youth ministry in your congregation?

Who should answer these questions? In many churches it will be a group referred to as the *youth committee of the board of Christian education.* In other cases the committee may have a different name, and it will, of course, take different shapes in response to each local situation. The basic assumption is that *each church needs a group responsible for establishing the church's philosophy, policies, and program in youth ministry.*

The makeup of the youth committee should include those who have adult leadership roles (teachers, advisors) in the youth-oriented structures of the church, adults who are concerned about youth (parents, other church members), and youth.

A word about the "and youth." Youth participation is essential in a committee concerned with youth ministry. Joint participation by youth and adults in a planning, decision-making body is a new experience for most persons. Old rules for committees are not helpful and do not apply. New personal and group attitudes and behavior need to be developed. (Appendix A offers guidelines for youth/adult planning and decision-making groups.)

SO —

1. If a group doesn't already exist, form one that assumes responsibility for youth ministry.
2. Whether it's a new or old committee, learn how to work together. You'll find *Team Building in Church Groups* (Geyer and Noll, Judson Press) a helpful resource.
3. Deal with these five questions about youth ministry:

QUESTION 1

What priority does youth ministry have in your church?

Is it really important? To what degree is the concern expressed "lip service" only? Or is the concern reflected in leadership commitments and budget appropriations?

Examine Your Leadership Commitment

- Determine the number of adults necessary for leadership roles in youth ministry in your church.
- Now double that number. (If you come out needing ten [teachers, advisors, etc.], make it twenty.) From a list of the total membership of your church, select the twenty persons most suited to give that leadership.

    Consider:

    Ability to model the Christian faith,

    Ability to communicate with youth,

    Skills in group work, planning, etc.

- When you have your twenty listed (and if you're doing this as a committee, you should get consensus on who the twenty are), identify those who are now involved in youth ministry. If there are some who should be involved but aren't, why aren't they?
- If you have a high percentage of those listed involved in youth ministry, then you're implementing your priority. If not, then you have some evaluating to do.

Now Examine Your Financial Commitment

Does the budget of your church make adequate appropriations to undergird youth ministry efforts?

- Are there funds available to assure participation of at least half of the adult workers with youth in as few as two or as many as seven days of training annually? Such training may be a laboratory school, a workers' retreat or conference, focusing on resources, methodology, or self-understanding.
- Are there scholarships available to ensure support for half of the youth on your roster for attending varieties of youth-oriented informing, training, or enriching events each year? (Camps, conferences, seminars of a church or nonchurch nature that provide for development of the person.)
- Are there funds available for program support? Can you charter a bus, buy some books, rent a film, purchase needed equipment, reimburse drivers for mileage — in short, pay for the tools that are needed?
- Could you fund an experimental ministry? If a help line or counseling service were needed, does your budget provide room to experiment with a new form of ministry?

- Does your benevolence or mission budget reflect a concern for youth service "ministries" in your community? Are you supporting counseling services, drug information centers, youth/adult encounters?

So, do your leadership commitments —
and your budget —
reflect your church's concern for kids?

If the chairman of the board of deacons is the best suited person in the church to work with senior highs but doesn't, why not?

If you're paying more for cleaning drapes and remodeling a rest room than you put into youth ministry, is your commitment to youth ministry established?

If these two illustrations describe your situation, then, to borrow some words from the game of *Monopoly*, "Do not pass GO. Do not collect $200. Go directly to jail!" You're in trouble!

QUESTION 2

How well have you interpreted youth ministry to your total congregation?

Does everybody have opportunity to know what's going on? Congregations are often kept in the dark about youth ministry events.

Check (✔) the category that applies to your church:

__ We feed our congregation public relations-type information that will insure unquestioning support, particularly financial support.

__ We don't say anything unless asked.

__ We make an annual report.

__ We seek regular opportunities and even schedule special meetings with segments of, or all of, the congregation to communicate and engage in dialogue on our goals, achievements, difficulties, and frustrations in youth ministry.

Obviously, you should have checked the last item. Checking the others doesn't mean you fail, however. It may mean you're very honest. But it does mean you've got some work to do.

Recognition of youth ministry as a *priority* in a church is directly related to the amount of knowledge about and concern for youth needs and possibilities that a total congregation has. ("Possibilities" imply youth's ability to meet their own needs and contribute to the church.)

Some Practical Steps

#1   Youth need to see themselves as a potential part of the total church.

#2   Youth ministry goals must be clear, or interpretation will be foggy.

#3   Interpretation must have a regularity about it, so —

#4   Publish a regular "communication" for the congregation.

#5   Meet with classes, boards, committees to share goals and plans.

#6   Invite non-youth (children and adults) to share in your planning.

#7   Communicate your goals!

#8   Tell what you plan to do.

#9   Do it!

#10   Report what you accomplish.

Emphasize youth/adult activities, for personal relationships are the best form of communication.

Your goal for interpretation might be that any member of the congregation can talk with any other member of the congregation about the philosophy, policies, and program of youth ministry in your church.

QUESTION 3

What assistance and support do you expect from the congregation?

My grandmother used to say, "Children should be seen but not heard." Some of us in youth ministry operate on this philosophy in terms of our congregations. They should be seen but not heard. Let's cool that concept — but fast. None of this "don't call us — we'll call you" kind of operation. Now that the people are aware of youth ministry, you need to listen to them!

If you have an established procedure for interpretation and your congregation is aware, what is it you expect from them?

Members of the youth committee (or other administrative group) need to indicate to the congregation the ways they can be supportive. Generally, the congregation needs to:

* *Undergird youth ministry* with spiritual, human, and financial resources;
* *Contribute ideas* that will implement the philosophy of youth ministry held by their church;
* *Provide resources* that are available to them and that they in turn can make available to youth ministry efforts (e.g., books, films, professional skills, a summer cabin).
* *Offer constructive criticism* that will enable youth and adult workers with youth to identify the strengths and weaknesses in their effort.

Remember these are some *general* descriptions of support. The congregation's support role needs to be described in terms of the specific efforts being made by the church. For example:

"We need your prayer support during this college campus tour we are making with our high school seniors."

"As you listen to youth talk of their recent experience in the drug education campaign in our community, what do you feel our next step might be in that area?"

The second illustration implies a congregational involvement in planning through the seeking of data and the testing of ideas. Your youth ministry committee may want to consider forming a "Youth Ministry Think Team," composed of youth and adults. The "think team" would be an informal group with responsibility for creative thinking but not for decision making and planning. Its role might be:

Brainstorming new possibilities;

Offering constructive criticism of what has occurred;

Responding to new ideas with reaction data that will determine feasibility.

The "think team" would serve to involve more persons in thinking about youth ministry and serve to bring it out of the dark, out of the "church basement" into the "parlor."

QUESTION 4

Does the youth committee have a clear understanding of what it expects of adult workers with youth and what the adult workers expect of the committee?

Most adult workers with youth "give up" because in the beginning they were sold a bill of goods.

"There's really nothing to it," the youth committee member told the "sweet young couple" whom the committee had decided would be "so good with the young people."

In a few short weeks the "sweet young couple" knew they had been taken. The youth committee didn't know what it was talking about, *or* they knew and wouldn't admit it.

"Sweet Young Couple" resigns!

It is essential that the youth committee describes with accuracy the demands that an adult worker will face in youth ministry. The demands will vary, of course, with the role (church school teacher, group worker, etc.) and in light of the church's objectives in youth ministry.

The youth committee needs to prepare an accurate description of the role of the specific adult worker. The description needs to include:

- A listing of the skills and/or resources the adult worker will need to offer (e.g., planning, being an enabler, listening).
- A realistic appraisal of the amount of time that will be required.
- A summary of training possibilities and an indication that participation in training events is a part of the role.

- A description of relationships to board or committees that are involved with the role described. (In some cases, the advisor to a youth group will, by virtue of that role, be a member of the youth committee.)

These are both the role description and the expectations that the youth committee has for adult workers with youth.

When adult workers are recruited, they should have the opportunity of indicating to the youth committee their expectations.

Expectations in both directions ⟷ can be shared in a work session. This review could be an annual activity of the youth committee and adult workers.

Working separately, each group should list their expectations for the other group. Put them on newsprint or a blackboard or make quick photocopies for all in attendance.

Discuss each expectation so understandings are the same.

Expectations can then be stated in a contractual form with the youth committee agreeing to respond to the expectations put forth by the adult workers and the adult workers agreeing to meet the expectations put forth by the youth committee.

The situation is now clear. We know what we expect of each other. If confusion or conflict does develop, we have a base to determine why. Were there expectations stated and agreed to that were not met? Were expectations *not stated* which have become the source of disagreement? If either does occur, it is hoped the problem can be responded to on the basis of the expectations, rather than personality, and solutions identified and agreed upon.

QUESTION 5

What role do youth play in planning and directing youth ministry in your congregation?

Perhaps the best way to stress the importance of this question is to relate it to the "departure" of youth from the church.

Youth want to have a stake in shaping events and decisions that have an influence on their lives. They will probably be the first to admit that they don't have all the answers. They do want to contribute those answers they have. They also feel they may have some answers that others (adults, possibly) don't possess.

When youth are blocked from this kind of participation, they "leave," actually or symbolically. Those who have left symbolically are often present for the "body count" but are generally indifferent, refuse to accept or carry out responsibility, and are often passively or openly hostile.

There are three groupings in which planning and decision making for youth ministry may take place.

1. *In all-youth groupings.* There are times when the situation would indicate that a group of youth (peers) can best respond to a particular need.

2. *In all-adult groupings.* There are matters, particularly in the area of the adult role, that may be dealt with most effectively by all-adult groupings.

3. *In youth/adult groupings.* In the majority of youth ministry planning and decision-making situations, it is imperative that both youth and adults share in the process through some mode of interaction. This participation may take the traditional form of so-called "youth representation" on the youth ministry committee. It may, however, lead to a new understanding of youth involvement. How about a "committee or council" composed of an equal number of youth and adults where decisions are reached by consensus and where there is no vote, so listening, negotiation, and working out a solution acceptable to and endorsed by all becomes very important?

We are unable to explore the answer to this question without our biases being apparent. *The largest part of planning for youth ministry must be done by an administrative structure that includes youth.* Their involvement should result in contributions that are readily identifiable by their peers and the adults in the congregation.

This sense of participation will be the greatest single factor contributing to an increase of youth's sense of being a part of the Christian community.

SUCCESS!

We cannot close this section without a comment about success. Everybody seeks success in youth ministry. The trouble we run into is that Church A often equates success with what has been accomplished in Church B. Church A sets out to do what Church B has done or feels a sense of failure for not doing as Church B has done.

Success cannot be assured by copying nor can success be determined by measuring what you achieve over against the efforts of another church. "Success" can only be measured in terms of goal achievements:

You determine needs in your youth ministry.

You set goals to meet the needs.

Your success rating is determined by your degree of goal achievement.

(See Appendix B for help in goal setting in youth ministry.)

Don't worry about the church across town, in the next town, or in any town. Set your own goals,

THEN

and only then

the "other church" can be of help to you (but not as the success symbol). Your neighbor may have tried some things which are applicable to your situation. Your neighbor's work may be of help to you if you ask, "Does the particular model or program used at Old First Church *give us some insight* as to how we might plan to meet our needs?" That's the key: see the other guy's work simply as an idea that you might *adapt* to meet your goals.

Watch out for the trap! Don't try things because they worked at Old First Church.

When at the end of the year you can
set off fireworks,
run up a flag,
join in a dance,
shout with joy
because you made *your* goals — that is SUCCESS!

2
Needs, Resources, and Response

Most youth ministry begins in September, at the time of the beginning of the new school year. Great plans are made!

The only thing we forget is that September's "kids" will be gone by November. "New" persons will stand in their places. We may be fooled, for the names and faces will be the same. But the ideas, the contributions, the concerns, the NEEDS (Remember the word!) will be different. The alarming and beautiful thing is that they'll be different again in January and February and June and so on.

In programming for youth ministry you must take that into consideration. *Change* is what you plan for. A three-week effort in group meetings or a mission effort of two-months duration may not survive for their planned time periods because of changing NEEDS within the group.

NEED is the word we should learn in youth ministry. Program must be developed in recognition of and in response to NEED. When programs meet needs, you'll find yourself involved in ministry with a significant group of young people.

Before we move into discovering needs, we should determine what we understand as the meaning of the term "program."

PROGRAM has traditionally implied an event or events that take place at a given time to entertain, motivate, or allow expression by a given group of people. Attendance at these programs has been largely based on loyalty to the sponsoring institution or its cause.

We are suggesting a change in the meaning of that term for youth ministry. *Program* is that which is developed as a response to the identified needs of a group of persons. Program grows out of an understanding of need and encompasses any and all responses to those needs.

If program means all that you do in youth ministry, then you will realize that needs can be responded to in a variety of ways and at a variety of times and that many kinds of responses are legitimate.

This recognition makes for a bit more comfort when you consider again the changeability of youth. You don't need to respond to everyone at the same time in the same way. You're free to respond to

> a variety of needs
>
> > in a variety of ways.

So, let's go after the business of discovering needs.

THE SEARCH FOR NEEDS

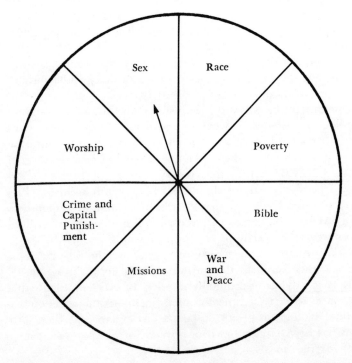

No, that's not really the way to determine need. Nor should you operate on the "What are we due to talk about?" theory. And don't make your decision on the basis of "the last time we talked about sex, we had a big turnout."

What you're after is an understanding of the ways that each

person related to your youth-ministry efforts thinks and feels about himself, others, and his world.

Following are four ways to identify needs:

1. Through an inventory by the adult worker with youth.
2. Through a group process.
3. Through individual interviews.
4. Through the testing of a proposed response to needs.

ADULT WORKERS' INVENTORY OF NEEDS

Adults who work with youth are obviously in a position where they can initiate response to needs. The form in Appendix C is suggested as a way the adult worker can discover, catalog, and plan for a program response.

It is but one form and can be utilized in whole or in part. The questions are examples of the kind of concerns that need to be probed. Ideally, the adult worker should do the inventory every three months, responding to all questions. The first round will be the most difficult. Later rounds will be composed, to a great extent, of updatings of earlier observations, comments, and decisions. Evaluation of previous observations is important in the later rounds of the inventory for purposes of understanding growth.

A PROCESS FOR GROUP DISCOVERY OF NEEDS

This process can be used by the committee on youth ministry, the entire youth group, a group of youth who are not an active part of the church's youth ministry, a group of parents or other concerned adults.

Questions to Use

Following are some questions you may find helpful. They *may* need adaptation for your situation. Or use them as guidelines for forming your own questions.

1. If you had the power to do anything in the world you wanted to do, what would it be?
2. For you to be a better person, what ideas do you need to explore?
3. What irritates you most about life today?
4. What are the things that are most important to you?
5. In your own words, indicate

  a. the greatest contribution that the Christian faith makes
     to your life today;
  b. the place where your faith lets you down.

Now try using these questions or your own in the following
process. Your purpose will be to motivate a group's identifica-
tion of needs. It is hoped that the persons who identify the
needs can also suggest suitable responses to the needs. In this
way, a group is helped to see what its needs are and what it can
do about those needs.

Step 1. Indicate to the group that you are going to suggest
some questions, the answers to which may give some indication
as to what they can do as a group (or what can be done as youth
ministry in your congregation).

Step 2. Suggest to the group a way of responding to the questions.

  • If the group is small (8-12 persons) and they can say to
    each other what they think, simply start a conversation and
    offer the questions one at a time.
  • If the group is large (12 or more) or does not have a high
    degree of familiarity among its members, use the following
    approach.

Suggest that in twos (each selects a partner with whom he or
she feels comfortable) they discuss question 1, making note of
their responses.

Second, they move together with two other persons and
share those answers to the first question that they feel they want
to share. Then in the group of four, discuss questions 2 and 3.

Move now to a total group and report those responses they
wish to share.

Now, as a total group, consider questions 4 and 5.

An alternate plan to this approach for a large group would
be to divide the group into groups of six to ten and discuss all
questions in those groupings.

Step 3. Once you have responses to the questions listed on
a blackboard or newsprint, tell the group that these comments
probably indicate some of the needs that we have and that we
can work on together.

Have the group look over the comments to see if some trends
appear. For instance, there may be a great many comments
reflecting loneliness, personal isolation, fear of relationships

which could lead to the observation that one of the needs is to "learn to know each other better."

Once a number of these are identified, suggest that every member of the group weigh them on the following scale:

5 very important
4 quite important
3 so-so
2 slightly important
1 not important

Total up the scores for each item. The item with the highest score is of top priority to your group.

Step 4. If time permits, divide into groups to discuss the ways of implementing the top three priorities. If not, appoint task forces to do this *in the next two weeks* and report back to the total group.

DISCOVERING INDIVIDUAL NEEDS

A third way to discover needs is to contact individual persons. Your purpose here is the same as in the group process: to understand how the person thinks and feels about himself, others, and the world.

Several approaches are possible:

1. Establish a consistent program, on the part of the youth ministry committee, of conversations, interviews, and so forth, of individual participants in youth ministry. Questions of the type suggested for use in the group process would be usable in these conversations, as well as questions of an evaluative nature. (For example, in what one specific way was our youth retreat experience helpful to you?)

2. Ask individual members to do some writing for you that would give you some insight as to need. Don't play games in terms of the reason for the writing. Make it quite clear that you are after their suggestions and insights as a help in ministering to youth in your church. Ask them, however, to write without consulting other persons. You want *their* ideas.

   Indicate that they may write spontaneously or you may offer for a beginning point an open-ended statement, such as:

   "If I had complete power to decide what our group

would do for the next two months, we would _____
_____."

If you take this approach, you will need to take time in the future for feedback to the writers and to reflect on their comments. It will be particularly helpful if you can point to ways in which their ideas have influenced planning.

3. Members of the youth ministry committee might invite two or three youth or adults who are involved in youth ministry to do some thinking together about youth ministry in an informal setting, such as over a meal. The conversation may utilize some of the previously suggested questions, or it may spring from some event or concern in the local community that involves youth.

Through the three processes just discussed, we are placing an emphasis on the personal nature of youth ministry. You are not simply working with "the kids" within the 12 to 18 age bracket or with "the group" but rather with a collection of individuals who happen to be in proximity to each other. When youth ministry includes this personal, individual approach, it is more apt to be "ministry" rather than "program."

PRESENTING THE PROPOSED PLAN

A fourth way to discover needs would be for the youth ministry committee, or other planning group, to present its plans to the total group.

In this approach you seek

Reflection   Feedback   Critique   Evaluation

and so on.

What you want to know is: Does the group see your plan as being helpful to them? Can they point specifically to ways it will meet or not meet their needs?

Most important, can each group member make a commitment to participate in the plan?

Approaches open to you are:

1. A sharing of the plan in the group session pointing to where you particularly want appraisal, but seeking a response to the total plan.

2. Preparing a questionnaire (data collector) with questions, the answers to which will verify or contradict your plan.
3. Asking several persons not on the youth ministry committee to meet with the committee and go over the plan.

Any of these approaches should give you information as to how well you're doing in meeting needs in your planning.

RESOURCES TO MATCH NEEDS!?

So the needs are known.

The second thing that you need to consider is available resources. Every church has certain kinds of resources for youth ministry. As your committee on youth ministry begins the process of guiding your church in a response to youth needs, they should create a realistic inventory of all the resources they think are available to do the job. A list might include:

1. The persons able to work directly with youth.
2. The funds the church budget can provide.
3. The kinds of rooms and facilities available.
4. The pastor's contribution.
5. The resources of other church members (career counseling, transportation, food service, medical assistance, listening, etc.)
6. Resources of the immediate geographical area (parks, retreat centers, colleges, etc.).
7. Community resources, organizations, persons, etc.
8. Churches with whom cooperative ministries might be established.
9. Other possibilities.

When the resource inventory is complete, the youth ministry committee should have a pretty good idea of what it can and cannot do.

There is little wisdom in a church overreaching its resources. This will only lead to frustration. The youth ministry committee in appraising needs should recommend responses that are within the possibility of achievement in light of resources.

The intersection of needs and resources

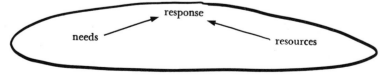

will indicate the specific forms of ministry responses open to your church.

RESPONSE

With this understanding, let's explore the varieties of ministry open to the church. Remember that when we talk of youth ministry, we talk of a ministry "to and with youth, in and through the church."

Youth ministry is a broad, evangelistic, mission-oriented concept that moves the congregation outward as well as inward in pursuit of its desire to experience the Christian faith with youth.

A "Nutshell" of Philosophy

In a nutshell, the philosophy of youth ministry means:

> You know the needs.
> You know the resources.
> You're free
>   of feeling there is only one way
>   to do it.
> You're free
>   to respond to youth in a variety
>   of ways.
> Your church's ministry can take any shape —
>   the necessary shape!

ALL THIS IS YOUTH MINISTRY — VARIETIES OF RESPONSES

Here's a church whose children are grown. Yet the adult congregation is concerned about youth. Still financially solvent, they secure a youth minister whose parish becomes the community, whose congregation is the youth and young adults of that community. That's good!

Some churches will choose to maintain the two most familiar approaches for youth ministry: church school and an evening youth fellowship. They make this choice because they believe the needs can be met there, and they have the resources to do those things. That's good!

Some churches need to go far beyond church school and youth group in their efforts with youth. Needs and resources dictate this. So, a strong musical program, mission and ministry trips, personal growth groups, a vocational counseling service for church and community youth, and in-depth task forces for response to social issues are all a part of this church's ministry. That's good!

And here is a church that is very small, with just a few youth, and so two things go on:

1. Weekly the pastor and the youth get together for talk or doing or seeing. No heavy planning, no great demands. They come together, eat, talk, see a movie, listen to a record, go somewhere to see a play, hear a prominent person speak.

This church believes in youth involvement, so the focus is training adults to enable youth to do their thing. The result: a youth-run "rap line" open daily noon to midnight, staffed by youth, enabled by adults. Weekly rap line training sessions meet the need for group life. That's good!

2. Once a month the church sponsors a community evening, sometimes a coffee house, sometimes a community activity, and that's good!

GROWING OUT OF RECOGNITION OF NEEDS AND RESOURCES

One of the important ways a church can be involved in youth ministry is by influencing the youth and youth-serving agencies of the community. A church may choose to do just that by dispersing its resources to strengthen situations outside itself. It might decide that its contribution to the community spectrum of youth service would be a counseling (individual or group) ministry, focusing on spiritual, moral, and ethical needs of the individual. That's good!

Churches need to get together. The only way for some churches to be involved in youth ministry is by cooperating with several other congregations. Each church may elect to do one thing "solo" so as to provide a continuing relationship to the home congregation, but everything else would be done cooperatively by a representative planning committee or

The cooperative model may call for each church to do one thing and contribute this one thing to the total group of churches. Either way, youth ministry may best happen in cooperative relationships, and that's good!

> There might even be a church that sets up task forces:
> - for biblical study,
> - for social action,
> - for creating forms of worship,
> - for personal growth.
>
> These compose the church's youth ministry, and that's good!

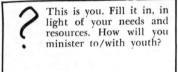 This is you. Fill it in, in light of your needs and resources. How will you minister to/with youth?

That's good!

IN SUMMARY

The youth committee has the responsibility of administering youth ministry in the local church.

The youth committee takes three steps in planning that ministry:

1. Determine the needs of the youth to whom the ministry is directed.
2. Determine the resources the church has available to meet the needs.
3. Decide upon the kind of response that needs to be made. This response will be youth ministry in and through your church. The ministry will be composed of one or many program efforts, all designed to respond to youth NEED!

3

Finding and Training Leaders

Your Question, Sir!
(Please answer carefully.)

HOW SERIOUS ARE YOU ABOUT OBTAINING
THE BEST QUALIFIED ADULT TO WORK
WITH YOUR CHURCH YOUTH?

Check one:

__very serious __serious __somewhat __only pretending to be

Please turn page upside down to evaluate your answer.

How serious are you about recruiting your best adult? Let's find out. What if the most qualified person in your church is a popular teacher of an adult class, chairman of a women's group, a board member, etc.? *Are you willing* to release him/her from the present involvement so he/she can be totally free for ministry with youth? What if this person is the pastor? *Are you willing* to redesign his/her work load so he/she can give a significant amount of time to working with youth?

THE KIND OF ADULT WE WANT

"foolin' around with our kids."
Number **One** criteria:
Simply stated!

The **Adult** we want working with our youth is the kind of person

who sees persons in the mob of a youth group;

who can **listen**, accept without judging, share his feelings, bounce back ideas, compromise when necessary, acknowledge his youth-maturity, stand his ground, know his **faith**, like himself;

who is a warm, compassionate, sinful, loving, hoping, anxious, serving, feeling man/woman of Christ.

IMPORTANT **? YES !**

But not as difficult as it sounds!
Just simple, plain, honest living —
the kind Christ talks about.

Sensitive ☑ Is person-centered — able to see the uniqueness of each youth as a person with problems, goals, concerns similar to his own.

Goaled ☑ Will want to have a sense of direction in his working with youth. May put the church "on the spot" when he asks and pressures them for their definition on youth ministry.

We could say

a lot more about the kind of qualifications that the PERFECT ADULT WORKER WITH YOUTH needs.

But we won't.

However,

We do suggest (and strongly so) that you sit down with the youth who will be involved with the adult worker you're trying to recruit and draw up a list of the qualifications they'd like this person to have. *Rank* them in terms of priority.

Compile a list of the adults who best fit those qualifications. *Rank* the names in order of preference.

Appoint a small group of youth and adults to *visit* the prospective adult workers. Always visit! *Never do the asking over the telephone!*

Why worry ABOUT A WHOLE LIST
OF CRITERIA WHEN YOU
HAVE ENOUGH TROUBLE
JUST FINDING ANYBODY?

BECAUSE

* An incompetent nincompoop will turn the present exodus of youth from the church into a flood;
* Youth cannot be convinced to "take seriously the church" when the church has failed to give serious consideration to an adult worker with youth.
* If no qualified person exists within your congregation, then you may need to consider the possibility of:
    (a) going outside the church membership for a competent adult worker;
    (b) curtailing some of your youth ministry activity;
    (c) clustering with another church or group of churches;
    (d) or ——

For the Adult Worker with Youth
What youth want in an adult adviser and the roles that an adult assumes when working with youth are usually the same.

GUIDELINES FOR AN ADULT WORKER WITH YOUTH

1. AN ENABLER-DEFENDER OF THE FAITH

— A climate of openness and honesty is a "must" for an effective youth ministry. Youth need to know that they can express positive/negative feelings without fear of reprisal, raise questions and doubts about their faith and living style, and seek guidance for family issues, etc. Too many of our churches fail to provide this kind of climate, "and the kids never come."

The adult worker will need to encourage this kind of atmosphere. He will seek to ENABLE open/honest expression among youth. He will then become an enabler/defender of the faith in that he will be seeking within his ministry the open, sharing fellowship of the early church. He will seek to awaken a sleeping people to their destiny as a living, breathing community of lovers—God's true people—young and old seeking to help and be helpful.

— He will work for the kind of experiences that will enable youth laity to discover the beauty of discipleship *as a reality*, not a discussion topic.

— He will recognize the fact

* that youth are to "minister to" as well as be "ministered unto,"
* that youth need to recognize and accept their responsibilities as members of a faith community which exists to serve the world as an expression of the continuous ministry of Christ.

But let's not scare you...
A Checklist of Other Criteria

Age ☑ Is anywhere between 25 and 65. (Age is not really a factor. Some of the oldest people around are between the ages of 15 and 18 years. Some of the youngest are 45 and above. Don't accept the stereotype that "only the young adult" can work effectively with youth.)

Time ☑ Must have a willingness to spend more than an hour or so a week for ministry with youth. Yet, he must be MATURE ENOUGH to be able to say NO when youth begin making too many demands on his time.

Adult ☑ Is aware of what it means to be an adult and reflects that image. He can make mature judgments. Is objective. Willing to face facts. Is not afraid of either youth or adults. He likes himself, his age, his place in life. He agrees with the young person who said:

> "We don't want advisors working with us who will use us as an excuse for them to become teenagers. We want adult workers who will help us become mature."

Disciple ☑ Has a significant understanding of how his faith affects his living. Is willing to share, but not browbeat youth into discovering the meaning of the gospel for their living.

Explorer ☑ Is free and flexible. Is willing to try new things, discover new directions, new ways of working with people and having people work with people. Yet knows when and how to establish limits.

Competent ☑ Has the ability to work with people. Has some group skills, but is willing to learn. Has some understanding of adolescent development.

Open ☑ Is willing to accept and use other people's points of views. Understands that youth are full ministers of the church, now!

YOU ARE CAPABLE OF ALL OF THIS!

2. MINISTRY WITH A PURPOSE

Specifics of your role include some of the following. You will be competent in some of them. Others may require additional training on your part.

A clock without hands ticks uselessly. A group of youth without goals and objectives drift aimlessly into

* apathy/boredom/sinking membership

* busyness without seriousness

* programs — programs — programs

* and other kinds of useless things.

YOUTH NEED TO SET GOALS FOR THEIR
ACTIVITIES AND MINISTRIES.

How?

a. GET your own ideas, dreams, and hopes into focus (writing).

b. ASK (and wait) for your board of Christian education to give a specific description of its youth ministry goals. The church generally has a vision (usually garbled and confused) of what it would like to have its youth become. The board should try to put this vision into specifics.

c. MEET with youth. They will have their own ideas of what they would like to be doing within the life of the church.

d. USING your own goals, the board's, and those of your youth, develop and write a specific set of goals which can be accomplished during the year.

e. BEGIN planning some of the things you can do to reach those goals.

See Appendix B for goal-setting and planning steps.

3. INVOLVING YOUTH

Youth must assume as much responsibility for their ministry as is possible.

Junior highs will need a lot of guidance in the planning and carrying through of their programs. They need to be a part of the planning process but will not resent adult initiative.

Middle highs on the other hand, will need less help from you. Yet your guidance will be needed to keep things moving. It's a strange age for these youth as they fluctuate from complete irresponsibility to extreme responsibility.

Senior highs can and will assume most of the responsibility for their life and ministry — theoretically. Be prepared (and accept the situation without coming to their continual rescue) for last-minute preparations, failure to show up, flops, and less than absolute perfection in program planning.

Hold on! When things can't seem to get any worse (they will), "one of those kids" will rescue you and your ego by providing one of the best planned and executed programs ever presented in the church. Senior highs will tend to view you more as a "resource person" than as a program/project leader and planner.

4. ADULT LEADERSHIP STYLES *See - Ditto*

How much freedom will you allow youth in the making of their decisions? How democratic will you be? How authoritative?

There is no absolute guideline except to say that people (youth) work better when they are a part of the decision-making process.

There are several styles of leadership, some of which work *best* all of the time.

Tells

The leader makes the decision and tells the group what to do. (He should take the feelings and needs of the group into account.)

Sells

The leader makes the decision and tries to sell it to the group.

Consults

The leader shares the issue or problem with the group and asks for their opinions. He then makes his decision.

Joins

The leader presents the issue, joins in the discussion, and abides by the group's decision. He becomes "one of the group."

Delegates

The leader presents the issue to the group for their solution or answer. He accepts the final result of their work.

Combine the preceding ingredients according to the situation.

You will use more than one in any given youth experience of which you are a part.

5. THE SOUNDING BOARD ROLE

The ability to "listen and hear what's being said" is one of your greatest roles. Play it well. Live it right!

* Youth do not mind an opposing view *if* their views have been taken seriously. They *appreciate* the chance to argue their point. They *resent* being treated as children with childish ideas. They *want* **you** to accept them as mature youth even as **you** want them to accept you as a mature adult.

* Be **patient** in your listening. A lot of "talk" may have to take place before the real idea or real feelings come through.

* **Read between the lines** Listen to more than the words being spoken. What are his eyes saying? What is the expression on her face? People are saying things to you by the way they sit, act, gesture, etc. *Learn to listen* with your eyes.

* **Your unconscious conversation** the way *you* sit, lean, gesture, hold your mouth, etc., are expressing your feelings toward the speaker. Be aware of your unconscious body conversation.

* **Say it** when you don't understand what's being said.

> I'm sorry, I don't think I understand. Would you try it again?

> OK. What I'm trying to say is—

6. "MY GROUP" SYNDROME

Do not make the mistake of seeing the group of youth with whom you are working as "your group." They are not. They are their own people! See them as such. Independent, self-seeking, self-giving, individuals. John, Jack, Bob, Beth, Michele. People with their own hopes, fears, aspirations, and failures. You do not own them. Nor do they own you.

* *Several groups in one.* Too often an adult will try to persuade (force) all of the youth in a group to do the same thing at the same time. Plan for variations and subgroupings based on personal needs and interests. A great variety of persons exist within a youth group. Discover them.

* *Don't overprotect.* Let group members find themselves. Enable them to assume responsibility for their mistakes and failures. Don't act as a shield between them and other adults in the church. Work for youth-adult dialogue, confrontation, reconciliation on a person-to-person basis.

7. A COMPASS

A large part of your job will be to keep small-group discussions "on the subject" and week-by-week activities in line with the goals and objectives which you and your group accepted for yourselves. Always keep in mind your long-range objective in order to have a ministry with purpose.

8. HUMAN RESOURCE

That's what you are — a human resource, the person who knows where to get books, films, resource speakers, etc., on any given subject at any given time. The youth expect more of you than you can give. That's OK. Let them know when you don't know. But to keep up-to-date, stay abreast of:

* latest movies (religious and secular)
* records
* leader's magazines
* local and national news
* regional and national training events

9. BEING YOURSELF

Youth appreciate genuineness and honesty in an adult. Be yourself.

* Admit goofs and mistakes; accept congratulations for things well done.

* Don't oversell yourself or your ideas.

* Use your own language; don't try to enter the world of youth. (You will never make it; you are an adult.)

* Don't accept church projects for youth that other church adults will not do (dishwashing, leaf raking of the church-yard, etc.).

* Don't praise youth for being young; praise them for the things they do as "individuals."

* Love yourself. Then you will be able to love them as youth, as persons.

YOUR FIRST STEPS

AS AN ADULT WORKER WITH YOUTH:

1. MAKE sure you read this book from cover to cover.

2. MEET again with the person who asked you to be an adult worker with youth. Share your questions and feelings.

3. REREAD the section in this book on the how and why of setting up youth ministry priorities (chapter 2).

4. MEET with your youth. Try to set up a weekend retreat as a long exposure experience. It will provide the time for you to discover who and what the youth are. And they will be able to size you up and anticipate what can be expected of you during the year.

TRAINING EVENTS

1. Your state denominational group will be offering several train-ing events this year. Plan to attend at least one of them.

2. Courses on adolescent development and youth culture are being taught in one of your local colleges or community night schools. Ask your church to provide your tuition fee.

3. Your denominational department of ministry with youth probably provides national training events. Check with your pastor for times and dates. Don't be afraid to ask for a tuition scholarship.

4. Your church should be providing some training experiences for those of you who work with youth. If not, ask them to do so.

4

Organization

It's fitting that we deal with organization at the back of the book. In youth ministry today, the question about organization should be the last one you ask. Let's diagram what I mean.

You start with a basic organization, the youth committee. It's an organization formed with a purpose — to plan for youth ministry in your church. The committee looks at needs, resources, and responses.

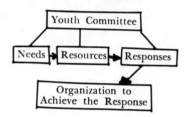

That's right! You organize *now* to achieve that which you have said you need to achieve — your responses to needs in light of your resources.

Because the tradition of "youth work" has often contained one basic organizational model that everyone could follow, I'm quite often asked to provide that model today.

In light of the needs-resources-response theory, I can't really do that. To say that every effort in youth ministry should have a president, vice-president, and several committee chairmen, or some other basic organizational form would be contradictory.

BASICS

There are some basic *qualities* that must be present in any organizational structure in youth ministry. I suggest that these *qualities* are the real basics rather than an organizational form.

These basic qualities are:
1. efficiency
2. flexibility
3. involvement
4. cross-generation composition

Efficiency suggests that your organizational form needs to set its sights on achieving its goals with a minimum amount of overhead. Don't get caught in the trap of officers for the sake of officers or offices to make people "feel involved." Select those persons who are most capable of helping the group achieve its goals. A team of five persons is probably the minimum working number for the generation of ideas and assumption of responsibility. A team of eight is maximum. Don't succumb to the mishmash of cumbersome titles, structures, and constitutions. Such entrapment means you spend all your time lubing the car and tuning the engine, but you never get out on the road.

Flexibility means you *can* change! Don't build an officers' empire — an elite corps of youth leaders who simply rotate themselves as the leadership group. This will stifle the interest and enthusiasm of other youth. *Everyone* needs a chance to lead and follow. Tenth graders need a chance to lead, according to their ability, and not wait until they are twelfth graders.

Flexibility means your organizational form changes according to what you are doing. A committee of five may be all that is necessary in the fall, but by Christmas the committee of five may be replaced by three task forces focusing on three distinct efforts of your church's youth ministry with two persons from each task force serving on a coordinating committee.

Flexibility means you see organizational change as an asset — not as a sign of failure.

> In the past you would say (with a long face), "Our group is not going anywhere. It's a dud. We need to reorganize!" Reorganization was an admission of failure. Phooey! The changing needs of people mean you have to organize in a different way to meet those needs. Structural change is logical and good. *It's okay to reorganize* so long as you know that *you are reorganizing to meet new, specifically stated, understood goals.*

Involvement means that those on a "steering committee" work to involve all the members of a group or project in shaping and implementing ideas. Projecting, planning, and doing are not the sole property of the committee.

The king/serf model of organization is really passé. Any committee that gets a "king complex" needs to be impeached. When a committee starts referring to the group members as "they," the king/serf model is setting in.

Leading a group is a "we" process. Whatever the structure (committee, task force, etc.), they need to think in the "we" frame of reference. It is the job of the "committee" to help something happen for the whole group — not to implant *their* scheme on "them."

A committee or task force needs to gather to itself the ideas, feelings, and needs of all the group and help all the group develop a sense of total involvement. "It's *our* thing!"

Cross-Generation Composition means that youth and adults need to be involved together in organizational structures. This involvement of youth and adults has too often been done in one or the other of two ways in the past.

1. The adults made all the decisions, and the youth were passive.
2. The adults abdicated and sat on the fringe while youth made all the decisions (in many cases, subject to phantom adult control).

What's needed in youth ministry is an organizational model that provides for the interaction of ideas and feelings of youth and adults in a setting where neither group dominates or abdicates. Perhaps the terms "arbitration" and "negotiation" give some direction. However, the most positive term may be "consensus." "Consensus" means that two or more points of view have been expressed and that neither group won or lost but that the total group reached a position that is acceptable to and can be endorsed by all involved as *their* idea or position. Such a style could bring theological experience and understanding into the organizational structures of the church, for such a model calls for an understanding of and deep respect for the other person.

Whatever the nature of the organizational structure, it must include youth *and* adults.

A BEGINNING

Now that we've described *some* qualities (there may be others), it may be safe to suggest a *beginning* organizational form usable by many churches.

The term "beginning" is more appropriate than the term "basic" in light of the need-resource-response philosophy. "Basic" implies a form that is commonly used by all churches. "Beginning" implies a form that is fluid and readily adaptable to the local situation. Here is a diagram of a beginning organizational form.

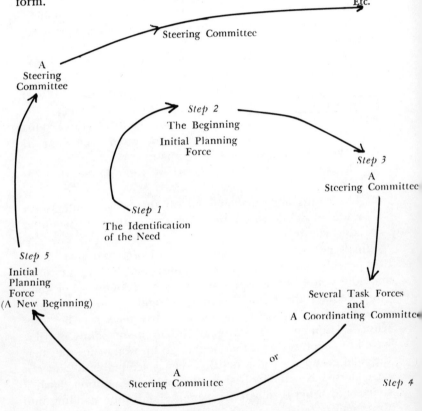

If the diagram confuses you, don't worry. Let's talk about what it means.

Let's assume that the basic organizational need in most churches is a structure for a group or an event. Let's also assume that:

> the board of Christian education and/or youth committee has called for the formation of a youth effort
>
> or
>
> the pastor and concerned parents want something to happen in the church's youth ministry
>
> or
>
> an adult couple are concerned about youth in the church and volunteer to start a youth group.

Okay?

Step 1. A responsible group, person, or persons have identified a need. A youth ministry effort (perhaps a group) needs to be established.

Step 2. The board of Christian education, youth committee, or pastor appoints an *initial planning force* composed of two adult workers with youth and four youth.

Their job is to:

a. Determine specific needs to be met.
b. Determine the goal or goals they want to achieve.
c. Devise a plan for meeting the goal or goals.
d. Do it.
e. Evaluate.
f. Determine, with the group or other persons involved, the next steps:
   - new goals,
   - revision of original structure to achieve those goals.

Step 3. Replace the initial planning force with a steering committee charged with implementing the new goals. They now repeat (c) through (f) in Step 2.

Step 4. Structurally this could be a repeat of Step 3, or a new structural form of task forces might come forth as the group matures and its efforts become more complex. The guidelines for work are still (c) through (f) in Step 2.

Step 5. Groups change! They often move from infancy and simplicity to maturity and complexity and then back to the latter as the group membership changes, as needs alter, and as the context of group life affects the group. So conceiving the structural form could once again become the initial planning force.

Now! Does the diagram make sense?

Needs evolve and change.

Goals (responses) evolve and change.

Structures evolve and change.

And that's the way it should be!

IN SUMMARY

Three things have been suggested in terms of the organizational structure of youth ministry.

1. Certain basic qualities need to be present in any organizational form.
2. A beginning form of organizational structure can probably be used by most groups and in most youth ministry efforts. The initial planning force followed by a steering committee makes the most sense and leaves natural openings for structural change.
3. We need to see structure as evolving, not repeating itself in a predetermined cycle, but evolving to that which is the logical next step in response to identified goals.

(Appendix B offers additional help on the relationship of goals or objectives to organization.)

5

Evaluation

Now that you've read the book, check here as to how you *feel:*

☐ confused   ☐ confident   ☐ in-between

☐ helped   ☐ full of ideas   ☐ discouraged

☐ encouraged   ☐ going to resign   ☐ _____

How you feel is important to us! If you have positive feelings, we feel good about what we've done and what it may mean to you and your church.

If you checked "going to resign," that gives us a feeling in the pit of our stomachs like

         ☑ sad

         ☑ what didn't we do?

         ☑ discouraged

Whether you feel good or bad at this point, we'd like to ask you to stay with us for a few more pages. It won't just be reading! We'd like you to do some thinking and writing.

Begin by responding to the directions in the box on the next page.

Write a paragraph (25 words more or less) that recalls your experience in reading this book. Describe what you thought this book was all about and what your feelings were as you read.

Now move to the next page. Read and follow the directions at the top of each column.

List at least three ways the book helped you! Ideas, sense of direction, a real learning for you, etc. Be as specific as you can.

List the things that you still see as problems — places where you need help in your youth ministry.

Write a description of your chief problem here.

How will you implement these ideas in your own church? How will they have an effect on your youth ministry in the next sixty days? Spell out those hopes here. Try writing them in goal form. There's help in Appendix B, item 3.

Now, let's try to solve that problem. To do that, write below a description of how you would like things to be if the problem didn't exist. Call this your goal.

You've got your goals. Now try for strategies and perhaps tactics. Use this column or other paper as a worksheet. See Appendix B for definitions of strategies and tactics.

Now! What are some things that you could do to reduce or eliminate the problem? Call them *possible* solutions and list them here. (As many as you can think of, okay?)

Goal

Strategy

Tactics

Which of all these solutions has the greatest chance of re-

Goal

Strategy

Tactics

ducing or eliminating your problem? Test the solutions by asking:

1. Is it something that we *can* do?
2. Can I commit myself to it?
3. Will it, more than any other solution, help us reach our goal?

Write a description of that solution here.

Describe your plan of action for implementing your solution. Action steps will include time and dates, people, place, equipment — all of the details necessary to implement your solution and achieve your goal (the way you would like things to be if no problem existed).

How do you feel now about your reading and thinking? Has it helped you to take some specific steps?

The left-hand column has tried to help you identify what you learned, what it can mean for your youth ministry, and how to plan for its implementation.

The right-hand column helps you deal with those problems that are still with you. It leads you through a limited problem-solving process.

We have done what we felt we could do in these pages. Can we risk a cliché as we close? A few words that kind of sum it all up (youth ministry, that is):

"Nobody ever said that it would be easy."

Appendix A
Guidelines for Youth Involvement in Planning/Decision-Making Organizations

1. The congregation should define what it means when it says "youth." A high school junior and a first-year law student both may be classed as youth, but their contributions may vary considerably.

2. The purpose of youth involvement in the planning/decision-making structures of the congregation should be clearly defined so that a fair evaluation of the contributions can be made. A clear definition of purpose might indicate that youth will:

    a. contribute new insights.

    b. share content and experience known only to their generation.

    c. assume responsibility in accord with their ability and experience.

3. A process should be designed which will enable youth to participate. Participation or involvement is not automatic or inevitable. The process should be aimed at helping youth and adults deal with change. Change will be necessary because these persons have not worked together in democratic structures where their contributions are seen as equal. Just as a golfer learns a new way to hold his putter to improve his stroke, youth and adults will need to learn new ways of conducting themselves in work groups in order to enable positive relationships to occur.

4. Training should be planned for the youth and adult members of the organization that will equip them to coexist in the planning/decision-making function. Such training would, for instance, equip the mature adult with new insights for:

a. handling his viewpoint and contributions, based on "years of experience";

b. freeing himself/herself to gain insights and new growth from the young person.

The benefits of training are not one-sided. Youth will be exposed to various models of adult behavior. These models will allow them to develop and test life-styles necessary to their becoming adult.

5. Adults should plan specific ways in which they can support youth's involvement in the planning/decision-making organization. A sponsor concept is a possibility. An adult sponsor would act as a guarantor for a youth member of the work group. "Guarantor" implies that he would demonstrate responsible participation in the work group and guarantee the right of the young person to move into that role.

6. The participation of youth should be placed in context for the youth participants. They should —

a. be briefed on the past history of the congregation.

b. be briefed thoroughly on the current priorities/concerns of the congregation;

c. be briefed thoroughly on the anticipations of the congregation related to their involvement;

d. be given a chance to explore the issues facing the congregation on their (youth) terms, while being encouraged to seek consultation from the whole congregation.

7. Consider the questions of youth-adult participation in the planning/decision-making process that may be unique to your specific congregation. For instance, in the case of churches that involve close family ties, what does it mean when you have a parent and child or a child and a close friend of the parent on the planning/decision-making body?

8. Some personal considerations must be made by all concerned of certain qualities of life, such as depth of sincerity, patience, willingness to change, etc.

9. Each adult member of the planning/decision-making organization must ask himself/herself: How would I feel if I were the only adult on the high school student council? What if, after a lengthy, all-youth deliberation on an issue, one of the youth turned to you and said:

"WHAT DOES OUR ADULT THINK?"

Appendix B
A Process for Establishing Goals in Youth Ministry

1. *Brainstorm Your Concerns and Needs*
   List anything on anyone's mind — no arguments, no debate; all concerns are acceptable.
2. *Refine Your Needs*
   Select the specific needs you can respond to in light of resources (time, personnel, money, etc.).
3. *Formulate Your Goal*
   The goal is your response to the need, what you intend to do about it. A goal is a clear, concise statement of intended outcome that will meet the needs.

A Goal Is: *Behavioral* — Change is anticipated.

Specific — It is not a general statement.

Achievable — It can be done.

Limited — It doesn't take in the whole world.

To Develop Goals:
1. *Look at the needs.*
2. *Brainstorm ideas* about the entire area of life to which the need relates. Do not discuss specific suggestions at this point, but merely list as many things as possible which could be part of the goal and could relate to implementation of the goal.
3. *Identify the ideas* presented which seem to represent workable goals.
4. *Rewrite the idea* into a clear sentence of intended outcome.
5. *Ask:*
   a. Will the goal really reduce the problem?

     b. Can I picture myself working on the goal?

4. *Design Your Strategy*

Develop a statement of what you intend to do to move toward the achievement of the goal.

    a. *Who* initiates the action?

    b. *Who* receives the action? For *whom* is it intended?

    c. *What* is the time span? *When?*

    d. *What* kind of action is planned? *What* do you intend to do?

5. *Develop Your Tactics*

Work out the details necessary to implement the strategy. How do you get the job done?

6. *Evaluate*

    a. Has change taken place? Have needs been met?

    b. Has the problem been reduced?

    c. What new concerns have been generated as a result of this action with which we need to deal?

    d. What needs can you now identify?

Other resources for planning:

Richard R. Broholm, *Strategic Planning for Church Organizations.* Judson Press, 1969.

John C. DeBoer, *Let's Plan: A Guide to the Planning Process for Voluntary Organization.* Pilgrim Press, 1970.

Robert Arthur Dow, *Learning Through Encounter.* Judson Press, 1971. (See especially chapter 12.)

Appendix C
An Inventory of Youth Needs

This form should be utilized as a confidential resource by the teacher for his planning purposes. An inventory should be done for each person in the group, class, or other youth ministry efforts.

AN INVENTORY OF YOUTH NEEDS

First Baptist Church
Anytown, U. S. A.

Name _____ Date _____

1. Respond to the question in each box on the left. Do the work and then read it over carefully, seeing it as a whole.

What friendship and peer group relationships does this person have?	What one thing do you think needs to occur in this person's life *now* to enhance relationships?

How does this person see himself/herself? What is his/her self-image?	What kind of steps should you take to: • reinforce his/her positive behavior? • help him/her deal with negative behavior?
What are the main concerns and attitudes that you have heard this person express in the last two to three months (personal, social, regarding faith, etc.) ?	Identify what you think is this person's chief concern and suggest at least two specific ways you can respond.
Where is this person in his understanding of a Christian life-style?	What needs to happen for him/her to continue his/her development?

2. Now respond to the questions in the boxes at the right in light of your comments in the left-hand box.

Respond to these four questions after filling out all eight boxes above.

What is the chief contribution this person can make to others, the church, and community in the next three months?

How can this person best be involved in the mission of the church in the next three months?

What is your goal for your relationship with this person for the next three months?

What implications do your discoveries about this person have for your church's total effort in youth ministry in the next three months?

3. In approximately two to three months this process should be repeated for each person related to your efforts in youth ministry. Before using this form for a second time on the same person, evaluate the efforts you have made. Be *particularly* concerned about how well you did in terms of what you said in response to the last three questions.

Evaluation

Since the last time this form was filled out, we have ___

_____

_____

_____

_____

_____